How to Draw a Blank

How to Draw a Blank
℗ Collin Van Son / Cathexis Northwest Press

No part of this book may be reproduced without written permission of the publisher or author, except in reviews and articles.

First Printing: 2020

Paperback ISBN: 978-1-952869-11-2

Cover Art, Design & Editing by C. M. Tollefson

Cathexis Northwest Press

cathexisnorthwestpress.com

# How to Draw a Blank

by
Collin Van Son

*Cathexis Northwest Press*

# Table of Contents

I.
| | |
|---|---|
| When Life Gives You Lemmings | 13 |
| Awareness | 15 |
| Now Here | 16 |
| Cloud Factory | 17 |
| In the Season of Dissection | 19 |
| Ravels | 20 |
| Preschool Cartography | 21 |
| Exorcist's Remorse | 23 |
| New Old Shoes | 24 |

II.
| | |
|---|---|
| Age of Incubation | 27 |
| New York City, 1929 | 29 |
| Fallout | 31 |
| notes from a woodburning | 32 |
| Bookmark | 33 |
| Oral Tradition | 34 |
| Rhythmia | 35 |
| Last | 36 |
| Jules Verne's 80th | 37 |

III.
| | |
|---|---|
| Cold Blooded | 41 |
| I Like My Cap with the Button-Up Flaps | 42 |
| Damage Sheet | 43 |
| Graffiti Above the Urinal in the DMV Bathroom | 44 |
| In Service | 45 |
| SPF | 47 |
| The Pigeons and the Treehouse | 48 |
| Playing God for Keeps | 50 |
| Ride Off | 52 |

*for Claire and Steve Van Son*

I.

# When Life Gives You Lemmings

Push 'em off a cliff.
We hadn't gone all that way
not to see their signature move,
a migration of such zeal
their brains run out of room to remember
what poor swimmers they are.

Back in Burbank, Disney watched the footage
and applauded our initiative.
He also asked to see my hand, which some say started
his whole cryogenics thing.

About the hand—

On the morning of our last day on the glacier,
the cold cracked our helicopter's "Jesus nut,"
so called 'cause if it fails
there's nothing left to do but pray,
meaning the documentary *White Wilderness*
would fail to contain any aerial shots
of said achromatic waste. Baited
by a lack of work, my naked hand
darted from its pocket
for a shake with the producer.
But instead of letting go,

he lifted it and squinted
at its pale, chapped back,
at the white-capped knuckles
with their inter-tendon valleys,
at the timberline of arm hair
fed by rivers of blue venous melt:
a perfect scale landscape
right at his fingertips.

About the shoot—

Close-ups of my clenched fist
for nearly three hours, my producer's boot
just out of frame, pinning my shivering
arm to the ice.

When at last we wrapped,
someone gave me a fur-lined glove.

Pulling it on
felt like nothing,
felt like
sticking my hand
in a lemming den,
or wherever it is
that they no longer live.

# Awareness

The telephone timber line spites the fall
of dying leaflets—*Missing: White Male
Pomeranian*—three-holed plastic sleeves
fogged with condensation, clean sheet reminders
that drawing a blank is the same as erasing.
Struck speciesless, the signs become possibly
the work of a woman whose husband followed
a map of his marrow
to northwest Poland, to a studio apartment
overlooking the Baltic, where he waits counting stone
and record skips. If you're going to lose
a pet or a father,
it's best if mom's a teacher
with access to the laminator
so you can post waterproof rewards
among sidewalk crack sunflowers
who cast their curbside shade on what aspires
to be sea glass. Collectors don't want
cuts or clarity, they want the moon
to erode so they can read
broken bottle messages. Pity the beach combers,
the homesick astronomers, stuck with seven seas
while their tidal-locked fathers lap
pools of tranquil nectar. The man who is pushing
a shopping cart cross-country
says he is doing it
to raise awareness. When I ask him for what,
he shrugs,
and pushes the cart into oncoming traffic.

# Now Here

It was at home, loading
clip after clip
about someone unloading
clip after clip,
that I realized we're lost.

But out here, snapping
tent poles into kindling
and building a pyre
of used magazines, I realize I also
don't know where we are.

And because I'm so tired
of dark and cold,
I will light my map as tinder,
will crumple this country
with its wilting compass rose
and kiss its edge with a matchhead.

I know, even before I begin,
that this will be my country's truest reading.
That the flame will show us
everything
as it slides 'cross the land like a finger.

After warmth will come the burning,
but first there will be comfort, comfort
in knowing we're all now here,
that empty space that beckons
from the middle of nowhere.

# Cloud Factory

During my year at the space agency
I opened each meeting with a reading from my horoscope
in hopes of connecting
via weakly correlated strands of red yarn
sunspot frustration and my bosses' average lifespan.

Instead I found that, left unchecked,
errant thoughts tend to bubble and congregate
in low-pressure zones like those above
surgeons' heads as they stand for concessions
in operating theatre lobbies.

With great glacial cleavings these proto-lightbulbs merge,
boil into cinderheads of thunderlit lilac.
It's suspected that brainstorms achieve peak violence
during El Niño, but the data's been elusive:
our best cloud watchers left for cybersecurity

where now they watch binary nimbi scud
through filtered blue and debate
if it's malware or a really weird duck.

Crossing a bridge on a seventh-grade field trip,
our substitute teacher pointed downriver
to the nuclear power plant's rising exhalations.
"Look," she said. "A cloud factory."
We knew it was a joke

but pretended we didn't—she was timid,
a stammerer, and our laughter
like so many carrion hooks

descended through whispers meant to be heard:
"She's supposed to teach us *science?*"
"I guess in her case the sub's for subnormal."

It was far too late by the time we noticed her
counting Mississippis like the silence after
lightning, growing larger and larger
as she shrank into the distance.

# In the Season of Dissection

Bleach-bright clouds hang in the dark
like contaminated icebergs afraid to melt,
watching the trees clutch their dying leaves.

Fall I feel dangerous in all the good ways.

I want to get punched
and also kissed, order TBD.
I want to tense anew,
as if I've never seen a see-saw.
I want to decode that bastard
of a postcard, torn in two
and ending with demands to *prove
the Earth is Your beloved.*

I want to come clean:

In all the years since,
I've never unwrapped a gift
with the same sense of promise
I felt toothpicking
through owl shit
to excavate a bite-sized skull,
acid washed to gumball white,
smiling in that special way
all choking hazards do.

# Ravels

A new frame's fallen every day this week.
Either autumn's branching into the inanimate
or the stickiness factor of my picture-hanging tack
is decaying with eerie punctuality.

It was 2 a.m., when the M.C. Escher fell
and I thought someone had broken in
and brought along their own pottery to break,
that I realized I needed to skip town for a bit.

The morning felt La Brean, bituminous.
I crossed the steaming street, felt the heat
of fresh-pressed asphalt as I waited
to be driven out, far and untethered.

Finding a seat by the bus's bathroom, I bound
my head in scarf, wound it around
like woolen gauze, and slept until we stopped
beneath a knotted overpass.

Once outside we diffused across the gravel,
the others smoking as I ate raisin bran
straight from the box. Columns of cloud
cast vitreous shadows like floaters in the eye.

Shivering in the wind, all I wished for
was someone to unravel me,
to dance with spinning ribbons
round the maypole of my mind.

# Preschool Cartography

Passing the playground, emptied for the evening,
I see it is littered with globe-patterned beachballs
slowly leaking captured breath.
They roll past the swings at the gentlest breeze,
mocking Atlas
with carefree buoyancy.

I love how toys feel simpler
when you throw out the directions.
Maybe I'm projecting here,
but when Mercator stared
at our ink-blue inkblot test
and ignored the poles altogether,
I think that spoke to his deep desire
to un-learn the truth about Christmas.

On the picnic table, leftovers
from snack or science class:
anyone who's smushed a Snickers
or reconstructed an orange peel
gets the gist of plate tectonics,
how schist and onyx
crest and encrust,
caking and baking
the continents' crust.

This thin skin sometimes pops, like the day Pompeii
froze in terra. History, as it happens,
is covered in dirt.
How many potter's wheels were smashed in protest
of the terracotta draft?
Did Scipio Africanus salt the earth of Carthage
as a compliment or curse?

Now more than ever,
the planet is a plaything,

every map of the world
a seven-piece puzzle
for Ages 6 & Under.
The pieces deny this,
deny it loudly,
but all you must do
is trace with your finger
South America's eastern coast.

Hold your breath and you'll almost hear
the muffled purr of homecoming land
when at last it comes to bury its nose
in the cove of Africa's collarbone.

# Exorcist's Remorse

There's a mattress lying dead
in the right lane of the highway,
the foam poking out lymphatic yellow.

Sunset, empty pizza box
a desk across my knees,
my bus lurches home
like a leaking aquarium.

I've learned to cook without
springing the stovetop trap.
Burners alight, the room smells of peanut butter,
softening bait.

With the right windows open,
the draft presses moths
into darkness, there to scrawl
remembrances in linen dust.

I clear them out on laundry day,
pinching their bodies
in used dryer sheets. Wadded and tossed,
it looks like they're resting
in scented cocoons.

Every time there's a newly chewed
hole in one of my shirts, I make up
my mind to buy mothballs.
And every time I do, I remember
the words of my landlord,
ex-proprietor of an ex-haunted house:
*The scariest thing a ghost can do*
*is leave.*

# New Old Shoes

An ambulance wails by,
and a big black wolf of a dog
harmonizes.

Losing a loved one is sad.
Loving a lost one is also sad,
which is to say it's all so sad.

I've finally acclimated to my sneakers.
I bought them used, the same style
you used to wear, so when I see them by the door
I wonder where you're hiding.

Olly olly oxen free!

They're a little big, but wearing them I feel
like running running running.

II.

# Age of Incubation

The vector was a mystery.
Fungus, virus, pigeons—
the city had no clue,
had no choice
but to quarantine its statues.

By morning they were sealed:
every garden gnome and gargoyle,
former mayor and famous player,
wrapped in tarps of sterile white
and duct taped at the base.

Though everyone averted
their eyes from the silhouettes
weeping condensation
down robes of gauzy plastic,
one nonetheless caught outlines shifting.

Walks in the park felt like showing up early
for a gallery opening, one where the docents
carried submachine guns
and forbid flash photography
from behind the barbed wire.

Rumors grew and split in two.
*They're searching for an antidote*
*in a lab within Lady Liberty's crown.*
*I hear Patient Zero*
*was a Terracotta Army vet.*

The end, as usual, was anticlimactic
for all those safe enough for story.
The weather turned; the blight lifted;
the soldiers sent back abroad.

You'd hardly know what had happened—

save for a few vacant pedestals,
the odd lonely plaque left blathering nonsense,

save for the mouth
of the bronze-bodied goat,
dripping with symptoms
of hunger.

# New York City, 1929

Though it's not yet snowing, passersby
anchored by empty bags and briefcases
stop in the street and tilt back their heads,
readying their tongues to catch a headline in the making:
*Another Broke Broker Broken.*

Children assure them that no two are alike,
these falling bodies, compound flurries
birthed in the inkwells of unbalanced books.

It's almost daily now: exsanguination
by way of missed payment and hit pavement,
sidewalks scored with back-break cracks

channeling snowmelt and other liquid assets.
Sewer grates sieve out the rest
for deposit in pine lockless boxes.


Forty stories up, the welder the crowd has mistaken
for a ruined investor preparing to jump
kneels in his plot of atmosphere
and steers a lightning splinter, Promethean glow
singeing the sky with incandescent snow.

Having met his wife in the shadow of a locked
and burning shirtwaist factory, the welder knows heat
as an instrument of union—his wedding is a weld seam,

a shiny, puckered graft,
commissioned in the burn ward, assembled in the chapel.
But gone are the days when sketches leapt to skylines.

*The arc torch gutters, the crescent hacks,*
*the moon closes early and the quenched steel cracks.*

The cloudbank finally chooses the speck of dirt
that will be its heart. Succumbing to the cost of growth,
the storm's first snowflake sings past the welder,

who whispers reassurance as he watches it go by:
*Forward! Headlong! All will be well.*

# Fallout

I can hear my sister sandpapering
over the kitchen sink. Her progress is slow—
the grain too fine—so I go to find her
something coarser. Down in the basement
our oil tank stands, bison-like on its four stubby legs.
Cat litter clots still crumble underfoot,
decade-old reminders of the sixty red-dyed gallons
that overflowed one winter night
and soaked the floor in diesel.

That spring our ferns all wilted.
A year later the birch stopped budding.
The hydrangeas, their flowers color-coded
to changes in pH, expired with a flourish:
cobalt to lilac, lilac to a bloody pink,
pink to brittle empty stalks.

In a cabinet below the taxidermied seabass
I find the good sandpaper
and bring it upstairs to my sister.
Her work is loud and fast now, the sound
no longer soothing as it smooths.
I haven't asked what she's making,
partly to distance myself from the mess:
even from here I know the wood's shrinking,
is raining dust like tired ash.

# notes from a woodburning

stove carry through the window
you opened to compensate
for radiator zeal

the breeze gives and
wakes from me a dream
in which the country's oldest theater
burned to the ground

burned to the ground
and took your office with it

staring at the smoke detector
waiting for its light to blink
I wonder if it has a light
or if it ever blinks

you groan and bury yourself
in blanket
I balance on the bed's edge
reaching for the corner of the ceiling

the standard test would wake you so I
kiss your forehead
and press a 9-volt to my lips
praying for its bite

# Bookmark

At one Minnesota library, winter ends
with the first snake of spring.
It's usually found in the reference section,
curled in the gap of a missing almanac, stranded
in yet another year
by blood too warm for sleep.

Context is everything: lose the book
and your bookmark's just a wasted ribbon.

These snakes—one wonders how they get inside,
or why they ever leave the den
and all their hibernating kin. But then,
who hasn't left the bed of one's beloved
for the company of Minnetonka's 1860 census?

1860: A hard year for the Samuelssons.
Two lost to typhus, a third to frost's bite.
A winter so cold they burned Bibles for warmth.

Their youngest daughter feeds the stove
another page, and the flame recalls
her sister's final lesson. By burning
sibling's gifted light, she begins to read.

Hello, Garden.
Hello, Mr. Snake.

Eyes stinging from the smoke, she
ties back her hair with a stray
scrap of ribbon,
blinks away tears
so she doesn't miss a word.

# Oral Tradition

The mountain breathes complicit snow.
The snow in turn cups limbless trunks
in white-wax hollows misshapen
by bent wicks and their spent,
senile gutterings. The moon shines clean
as a bone. Down in the valley
the townspeople wait,
in half-timber houses scrolled and embossed.
They peer through lattice windows,
out from the jaws of their icicled eaves.
Eventually it all will melt, like memories
of icing laced cross a hotcake.

> *Lost in snowy dark, the old huntsman's failing eyes chance upon a cottage.*
> *Inside, a pot of butter simmers, a pudding goes ignored,*
> *a bedridden widow pulls back her woolen covers. Gratefully*
> *the huntsman unlaces his boots and leans his axe in the corner.*

> *Afterwards, her appetite appeased, the widow will swallow him whole.*
> *She will treat their children with renditions in growled falsetto.*
> *She will curl up nightly beneath a rocking chair. She will spin lore*
> *while our teething ancestors chew the throat of their father's axe.*

Still we carry fabled truths.
To catch a witch, follow her nose.
Better yet to burn the bread,
eat the crumbs, erase the trail.
Tonight it is all coming back,
as one by one we reach for shears
and heft our gut-spilled cobblestones.
In towns of wood and sugar glass
the people splinter sweetly.
Snarl and gnaw, O oral tradition,
you taught us we were wolves.

# Rhythmia

A winterlong drumbeat:
the dog chasing rabbits,
squirrels, and chipmunks
through overgrown undergrowth
and out across the pool tarp, taut
like a drying hide.

Late spring we peeled it back
like burn ward nurses, pausing
to peek at the damage: swollen shadows
at depths assigned by density—
rabbits, squirrels, and chipmunks,
nestled in their brimming den.

Summer I spend poolside
while the sunroom swallows
finches, trapping them in self-reflection,
drums in their chests
growing louder and louder
as if that could stop the song from ending.

# Last

The microwave timer
counts seconds to extinction:
a sign at the store labeled this Lean Cuisine
the last of its kind, falling sales having sent
Asparagus and Cheese Ravioli
the way of the passenger pigeon.

Buried back-page obit
on my newspaper placemat:
the last male northern white rhino
passed away Monday in a Kenyan conservancy,
setting his daughter and her's adrift
in a gene pool too shallow to swim.

In gleaming labs, the scientists are watching
reruns of *Jurassic Park*. Fanfare drowns
out the stickered fridge, home to liquid lineage
in vials of four-letter
alphabet soup. Outside, mother and daughter
wait like sundials, horns casting shadows
that only count down.

# Jules Verne's 80th

Exploring's just searching
for what you cannot name.

Call it direction, a compass aspin:
no up, down, or under.

Call it three blank pages at the end of a novel
that somehow nobody fills.

Call it a dirigible—untethered, unfettered,
slowly sinking up into the fog.

Call it meaning, or respite from meaning.

Call it daylight if you're moving east,
darkness if you're moving west,

though, like nitrogen in blood,
distinction bubbles off

once you reach the core
and find neither light nor plesiosaur,

just hot dense nickel
where once you dreamed of a hidden sea.

III.

# Cold Blooded

The three of us wrote hate mail
while the other kids played Jenga.
I, the budding herpetologist, drew a man wrapped
in terror and in snake, the snake a ball python,
same as Sydra, who had just moved in
to the tank in my room where she'd live for ten years
before catching a parasite from her weekly mouse.
She died in corkscrews, the winter ground graveproof.

For street address we just wrote *Cave*,
and when Ms. Cantle asked our pen pal's name
we told her Osama bin Laden.
After locking our letters away,
she asked if we knew what had happened
on Tuesday.

Of course I knew.
Tuesday was an in-service day.
Tuesday I went to the zoo with my mom.

In the reptile house, cool and dark in those last days
of summer, a keeper's hand
opened over the desert
and rained hibiscus on the wrinkled *Uromastyx*.
In rapture I watched the smallest lizard
pinch a bloom in his jaws, all gum
but for one white speck: egg tooth,
escape hatch,
first world breaker.

# I Like My Cap with the Button-Up Flaps

It makes me feel like a bush pilot's mechanic,
though I suspect bush pilots are their own mechanics:
you can't just pop into the shop when the prop cuts out,
and if your pontoon breaks loose the best you can do
is make it a canoe, remembering to lash yourself
down before the rapids.

Today, my parents sent me $700
as if to prove the Yukon could kill me.
Long-johned and bath-robed,
I sweat my way through a pot of coffee, stopping
by the bathroom every so often
to squint and pick at my face.

Later I walked where the sky spat leaves
at the blue mirror lake, presumably so all would know
which was reflection. Jaw hinge creaking,
I skipped concrete shards till my fingers went brittle
and numbness overcame me in the abstract and concrete;
I felt myself slipping beneath windswept wreckage
until happily I remembered that my hat has flaps.

## Damage Sheet

Stapled to the last
page of the lease,
it shows what I'll pay
for all that I break:
$25.00 for the hole I cut
in the screen door,
$7.50 for the slat I snapped
watching you
leave through the blinds.

I wish at the start you had left
one such sheet
on my pillow,
though I doubt it'd have done
any good:
the fees feel so distant
on move-in day.
It's not till you're sleeping
on scuffed hardwood

that you realize
why making something habitable
is called
breaking it in.

# Graffiti Above the Urinal in the DMV Bathroom

*I STILL DRINK AND DRIVE* and below that
*ME TWO* and below that
*ME 3* and below that
my shoes, covered in piss

'cause I'm shaking so bad
and now it's Christmas Eve and I'm nine again
stretched across the backseat of a milk-gold minivan
winding with the Schuylkill on the way to Midnight Mass

across the river all drifting scabs of ice
loom eight blinking steeples
of steel tress and cable, soothing the valley
with red, asynchronous bulbs

the radio plays to silent night
I rest my cheek on the cool of the window
Kelly Drive throws another curve
and oncoming lamps glow warm through my lids

I open to the bleating
of bathroom fluorescents
high above the towers sing
wringing out their invisible light

# In Service

My mom, along with the rest of the K-5 staff,
has just been trained as a combat medic.

The gym teacher's embarrassed by his own disappointment;
until last week's in-service day he was the only one
with a stopwatch, wore it proudly round his neck

like it was whatever medal they give you for helping others
earn their own Purple Hearts—for lack of a better name
let's call it the Presidential Physical Fitness Award.

But thanks to a PowerPoint titled *Stop the Bleed*
every teacher can now tie a tourniquet,
and in each of their desks sits a stopwatch;

on slide six, in bubble-lettered WordArt:
lifesaving pressure, held too long,
will turn a limb necrotic.

After a Q&A that ran twice as long as the talk
everyone got a take-home prize, lanyards
embroidered with the 1, 2, 3's
of crisis response: Run, Hide, Fight.

When my mom asked what to fight back *with*
her colleagues surveyed the room for suggestions.
A yardstick. Safety scissors.
Cans of soup from the food drive collection bin.

The gym teacher perked up at that one.
A last-stand bombardment of split pea and chowder?
Sounds like dodgeball.
Sounds like a food fight.
How's your arm?
How's your aim?
Any food allergies?

Even if you miss
it'll help to have a mess.
When it's over we can hug our kids
and say it's all tomato bisque.

# SPF

An unbandaging: my father and I
peel back the tarp, exposing in stages
the stagnant water in its plaster bowl.

During a smokeless break in the shade
he points out the third of a lung he'll be losing.
From behind a sawgrass curtain the pool pump

aspirates, choking on a winter's worth of clotted
air. This was back
when he slept on his side. The body hates a crawlspace;

his went on to flood its newfound vacancy
with a fluid he claims to feel at night
pressing on his heart.

Two months post-op, on a white sand beach
in Sint Maarten, a red heat
blossomed on his back, irradiated butterfly

hovering in the shadow of his petal-plucked lung.
My mother wept at its shape. *A heart*, she said.
*Dear God, thank you. It's a perfect heart.*

Summoned from the waves, my sisters and I
squinted at the burn, my mother
hugging us in turn as she told us to give thanks

for his protection. Head bowed, I wondered
who had aimed the sunscreen so poorly,
or if my father's body was simply ripe for symbol.

# The Pigeons and the Treehouse

Short on wood, the treehouse half complete,
our eyes turned to the pigeon coop.

We'd risked our necks for those birds, scaled
behind the scenes at the drive-in screen

and plucked a dozen fledglings
from summer's crooked elbow.

They grew to be tumblers,
would soar to a speck then seem to slip

from the rungs of Jacob's Ladder, plunging
end over end till little Victor gasped

and they skimmed the tips of the citrus trees.
They were fun, the birds, but Vic's birthday was coming

and he'd always wanted a treehouse. So we scrapped
the coop, loosed the pigeons in the park

and discovered they were homing pigeons.
But now with no home to home to,

just a treehouse where they'd perch and shit
on anyone who tried to join. Having lost a brother

to avian flu, Pop was worried they'd get Vic sick.
So early one morning we went out and—

My father pauses at the apex of his story
and tilts his head at a sound from the kitchen.

It's my Uncle Vic, crying at how much
he'd loved that treehouse, at how much it'd hurt

when the birds disappeared
without teaching him to home.

# Playing God for Keeps

Knowing wet sand builds taller towers,
the kid next door liked to piss in our sandbox.

That was the year my teacher quit stars cold turkey
and dressed the best tests in Poison Control stickers,

the year I named my turtles Red Eye and Long Neck,
which, if not clever, would at least have been useful

had their namesakes been exclusive.
One of them—Red Eye, I think

(he had a slightly longer neck)—
liked to escape their outdoor pen

and hide beneath the neighbor's upturned canoe.
I tried to talk sense as I carried him home:

*Listen, friend. I know aluminum's shiny and sleek,
but that old shell is fused to your spine.*

June brought cicada killers
eager to earn their names.

I slaughtered them daily—it was the only use
those badminton racquets ever got.

They never stung people, but I didn't feel the need
for an excuse

until much later, drunk in late-July grass,
watching my girlfriend cry after shouting at her

for stepping on a bee.
That night, her sleeping hand open on the pillow,

the moonlight through my broken blinds
set aglow five pools of polished keratin,

compound of fingernail and shell, reminding me
of the summer Red Eye escaped for good

and I went into the woods to let Long Neck go,
his armor dabbed with a scarlet herald

so if we met I'd know his name.

# Ride Off

The old woman lost her fear of flying
around when she learned the adjectival form
of *terminal*. Today's in-flight movie
is a slow Spaghetti Western, closed captionless,
dialogue too dubbed to lipread.
She watches the backgrounds instead, comparing them
to the landscape below. Parkinson's joggles
her ginger ale. "The West's fastest hand,"
she jokes to her neighbor, left gripping right
as she dabs another spill.

Even now she still thinks in metric.
All *her* cowboys wear 38-liter hats,
plenty enough volume in which to drown a squirrel,
though her birdseed-stingy husband
had always preferred the rain barrel. He too was a believer
in conversion. Over the Atlantic in a Douglas DC-6,
wife of two weeks shaking with home/air sickness,
he'd busied himself with the math: at speed,
hugging the 70th parallel, a plane such as this
could bathe in lasting twilight, could keep the spill-prone sun
forever in its sight.

The fear may be gone, but it's not till they hit turbulence
that the woman truly relaxes. Shaken from outside
and in, the aircraft bucking with a frequency
in perfect opposition to the rhythm of her tremors,
she finds herself steady for the first time in years.
The drink cart crashes. Overhead luggage rains down in bursts.
The woman doesn't notice. Alone, still, utterly
secure, she sees something hidden
in the corner of the frame.

There it is,
hanging high above our heroes

as they ride into the sunset:
a jet plane vapor trail,
glaring incongruity that ruins the ending,
turns it into something
you can't really call an ending at all.

Collin Van Son graduated from Penn State University in 2018 with a degree in physics. His senior thesis, a short story collection titled "If You Don't Laugh, You Cry," was awarded the Henry W. Sams Award for Best Creative Thesis. 2018 also saw the world premiere of *TARVA*, an original play he wrote and directed with Penn State's No Refund Theatre, for which he received the organization's Best Director Award. His poetry has appeared in *antilang.*, *Typishly*, and *Cathexis Northwest Press*, and several of his plays can be found on the National New Play Network's New Play Exchange.

Also Available
from
Cathexis Northwest Press:

<u>Something To Cry About</u>
by Robert Krantz

<u>Suburban Hermeneutics</u>
by Ian Cappelli

<u>God's Love Is Very Busy</u>
by David Seung

<u>that one time we were almost people</u>
by Christian Czaniecki

<u>Fever Dream/Take Heart</u>
by Valyntina Grenier

<u>The Book of Night & Waking</u>
by Clif Mason

<u>Dead Birds of New Zealand</u>
by Christian Czaniecki

<u>The Weathering of Igneous Rockforms in High-Altitude Riparian Environments</u>
by John Belk

<u>If A Fish</u>
by George Burns

<u>En Route</u>
by Jesse Wolfe

*Cathexis Northwest Press*

www.ingramcontent.com/pod-product-compliance
Lightning Source LLC
Chambersburg PA
CBHW030139100526
44592CB00011B/963